Dedicated to

My personal savior

Jesus Christ

First EditionA

ISBN 9781795160278

CONTENTS

A Good God

When you are in a mess how do you view God?

Do you see Him looking down on you coldly while you suffer?

Is He sitting on pins and needles, biting His nails waiting for you to say just the right prayer so He can finally swoop in and rescue you?

Or maybe He is stroking His long white beard, analyzing your puny attempts to squirm out of your problem while He takes notes for pleasure?

Well, you may say "of course I never…." Never what? View God as mean, cruel or indifferent?

I'm willing to say that I too have had these similar thoughts. When I am hurting and being refined by fire, and I feel I can't take one more flame, these thoughts bombard me.

While I'm not proud to view God this way, I feel it's necessary to share this struggle. I also must say that these thoughts are LIES!

Logically these thoughts might seem to make sense. For example, let's say you just welcomed your first baby into the world, then you lose your job, you can't afford your house, and you lose that too, then you go to the doctor and get a horrible diagnosis of some sort. The whole while you are a faith-filled, Jesus following, believer. What else are you to think of God? Can He really be good?

My goal in writing this short book is to paint a picture of what the bible says about our Good Father. He is a true hero!

Mine eyes are ever toward the LORD *for he shall pluck my feet out of the net.*

Psalm 25:15

When you get to the end of this book, I want you to feel confident that the God of Abraham, Isaac and Jacob is a caring father, a devoted creator and a hero to all who love and follow Him.

Now I didn't say a hero to ALL! The Lord is a righteous judge, and there is no darkness in Him. Therefore, He rescues those who humbly accept His help and follow him.

¹⁷ The LORD is righteous in all his ways and holy in all his works.

¹⁸ The LORD is nigh unto all them that call upon him, to all that call upon him in truth.

¹⁹ He will fulfil the desire of them that fear him: he also will hear their cry and will save them.

²⁰ The LORD preserveth all them that love him: but all the wicked will he destroy.

Psalm 145:17-20

The Lord Shut Them In

I'm sure all of us have imagined one time or another what it must have been like to be Noah. Building a huge boat while the whole town watched for years in unbelief.

This would have been a humiliating process at times, yet Noah loved and trusted the Lord. He believed God's word that one day that boat would save him and his family from destruction.

Our God loves to save those who trust and love Him. When we are in trouble, He has asked us to call on Him. He asks us to be persistent in prayer and when we ask for something, He wants us to believe that what we ask will be given to us.

Therefore I say unto you, What things soever ye desire when ye pray, believe that ye receive *them*, and ye shall have *them*.

Mark 11:24

Noah teaches us that we should listen when God warns us of danger. What if Noah had ignored God? Would the human race have continued at all? When God warns you it's because He is keeping you safe.

So, we see here that God not only wants to rescue those who love and follow Him but also to prevent danger even before it begins. I'm sure the people in Noah's day were warned about their sinful lifestyle. God had planned for mankind to live in paradise in the Garden of Eden. He never wanted man to know evil at all. Before the fall of man when Adam and Eve ate from the forbidden tree of knowledge of good and evil, they weren't even aware of a life without their creator God. Then after decades of living apart from God, the world became so full of corruption that only Noah was serving the Lord and no one else.

God would much rather warn you that you are making a mistake than save you from it once it consumes your life with misery. Yet many times we brush off the warning and continue on our own path. Then even after we say "Sorry God, I know you are trying to help me, but I'm going to do my own thing and see if it turns out better. Sure, you're the creator of everything, but I got this, thanks!" He is still willing to help dig us out of the pit that we fall in. The pit He tried to keep us out of.

After Noah built the ark, God gave him seven days to gather the animals and his family and get inside the boat.

And they that went in went in male and female of all flesh, as God had commanded him: and the LORD shut him in.

Genesis 7:16

Maybe God shut the door to the ark instead of letting Noah do it to protect Noah from himself. If you were in the ark and heard people outside screaming for help you would surely want to open the door and bring them in. Sometimes God closes doors in our lives for our own good. The main thing to see here is God warns, He saves, and he protects!

God did not cause mankind to live sinful evil lives, man chose that. God did not want to end humanity, He wanted to save it. The only person who still followed the Lord was Noah, and the Lord cared for him and his family and saved them!

He can do this for you too if you will listen when He warns and call for Him when you are in need! Then believe He will hear you and don't doubt and know that He loves to protect and care for His children! That's who God is!

²⁰ Come, my people, enter thou into thy chambers, and shut thy doors about thee: hide thyself as it were for a little moment, until the indignation be overpast.

Isaiah 26:20-21

For the Sake of Ten

We are so unique in the eyes of our creator. He takes pleasure in His creation. He says He knows every hair on our head. He sees when a sparrow falls to the ground, and we are worth much more than a sparrow. This is why He wishes non to perish!

In the story of the destruction of Sodom and Gomorrah, a wicked land, Abraham pleaded with God to spare the righteous and not lump them in with the wicked. First Abraham asks if there are fifty righteous people in the cities, would God spare the land. Abraham then asks if there are forty would judgment pass. Then if there were thirty, then twenty, then for the sake of ten would it be spared.

God agreed!

Unfortunately, in both cities, only Lot, Abraham's nephew living in Sodom, was found to be righteous. When angels came to warn Lot to leave his home as destruction was coming, Lot attempted to plead with his sons-in-law, who were betrothed to his two daughters, to flee the cities with him. The men scoffed at him and laughed, they didn't believe him and would not come. This reaction shows the heart of the people. So only Lot, his wife and his daughters fled. Not even ten righteous were found.

The angels insisted Lot leave quickly, but he didn't exactly want to go.

¹⁶ And while he lingered, the men laid hold upon his hand, and upon the hand of his wife, and upon the hand of his two daughters; the Lᴏʀᴅ being merciful unto him: and they brought him forth, and set him without the city.

Genesis 19:16

This verse shows the nature of our loving, heroic God. Even when we resist in childish naivety, God will take our hand and lead us to safety. Are we deserving of this mercy? Does the creator of the universe have to gently care for each one of us? He doesn't have to, but He does!

The Pit

Many times, when we are in a situation that is difficult, we feel like it will never end. It can feel like we were thrown into a pit and left there. Joseph was literally thrown in a pit by his own brothers and left for dead. Then later he was taken out only to be sold into slavery.

When we are in a pit, where is God? That is what we often ask.

Does He see us? Does He care? And the big question, did He throw us in?

I have struggled with these questions, and I find answers in the story of Joseph.

So where is God when we are in a trial?

He is very close especially when we are hurting.

18 The LORD is nigh unto them that are of a broken heart; and saveth such as be of a contrite spirit.

Psalm 34:18

He's not far off looking down on us as we try to climb up the walls of the pit. He's in the pit with us. He's comforting us and calming us with his gentle voice. He's strengthening us with His mighty hand.

When I am in a mess, my first reaction is to struggle hard. I search every means possible for a way out. I research, I dig, I fight, and in the end, I am exhausted. Instead of trusting God, I trust in me.

This reminds me of when Jesus slept in a boat being tossed by a wild storm.

35 And the same day, when the even was come, he saith unto them, Let us pass over unto the other side.

36 And when they had sent away the multitude, they took him even as he was in the ship. And there were also with him other little ships.

37 And there arose a great storm of wind, and the waves beat into the ship so that it was now full.

³⁸ And he was in the hinder part of the ship, asleep on a pillow: and they awake him, and say unto him, Master, carest thou not that we perish?

³⁹ And he arose, and rebuked the wind, and said unto the sea, Peace, be still. And the wind ceased, and there was a great calm.

⁴⁰ And he said unto them, Why are ye so fearful? How is it that ye have no faith?

⁴¹ And they feared exceedingly, and said one to another, What manner of man is this, that even the wind and the sea obey him?

Mark 4:35-41

When I'm in a pit, I think of this story and all of a sudden it hits me that I could be sleeping next to Jesus instead of running my self ragged. I much prefer the first option.

Back to Joseph.

His life had taken a sharp turn for the worst. He went from a beloved favourite son to a slave and then a prisoner in jail for a crime he didn't commit. For years he was trapped in a situation he couldn't fight his way out of. His only hope was to trust in God and rest in the knowledge that God was faithful! Joseph had known the stories of his forefathers and how they had been rescued time and time again by God. He knew he served a God that saved those who followed Him.

So, does God see us in our pit and if He does, does He care?

29Are not two sparrows sold for a farthing? And one of them shall not fall on the ground without your Father. 30But the very hairs of your head are all numbered. 31Fear ye not therefore, ye are of more value than many sparrows.

Matthew 10:29–31

If every hair on our head matters to God, then yes, He sees us, and yes, He cares. If He notices every sparrow that has ever fallen to the ground in all of history then He is not caught unaware of whatever situation we find ourselves in. Later on, I will discuss the character of God to further emphasize His compassion towards His children. I must repeat that God takes care of those who accept Him and call on Him in times of trouble. If we choose to reject Him, he will not force Himself on us. He is not in the business of creating robots who are forced to love Him. That is why I must reiterate that Gods mercy and deliverance is for those who want it and those who want Him.

To even more emphasize this point this verse is helpful.

[17] For God sent not his Son into the world to condemn the world; but that the world through him might be saved.

[18] He that believeth on him is not condemned but he that believeth not is condemned already because he hath not believed in the name of the only begotten Son of God.

John 3:17-18

So, we see here Jesus came to SAVE THE WORLD! Whoever believes is saved! Whoever does not believe stands condemned. The help is a free gift all you need to do is accept it.

Now the last question you may ask when going through a trial is,

did God toss me in the pit Himself?

Well, let's look at Joseph as a good example.

2 These are the generations of Jacob. Joseph, being seventeen years old, was feeding the flock with his brethren; and the lad was with the sons of Bilhah, and with the sons of Zilpah, his father's wives: and Joseph brought unto his father their evil report.

3 Now Israel loved Joseph more than all his children because he was the son of his old age: and he made him a coat of many colours.

⁴ And when his brethren saw that their father loved him more than all his brethren, they hated him, and could not speak peaceably unto him.

Genesis 37:2-4

²³ And it came to pass when Joseph was come unto his brethren, that they stript Joseph out of his coat, his coat of many colours that was on him;

²⁴ And they took him, and cast him into a pit: and the pit was empty, there was no water in it.

Genesis 37:23-24

So, who threw Joseph in the pit? His brothers did, out of jealousy.

We know now that God was with Joseph and that He cared greatly for Joseph. Now we see He wasn't the one who put him in the pit. God did not send trouble your way. He did not toss you in a pit ever. These things happen because of the state of the fallen world! God only had good plans for Joseph and for you.

We can use these questions as tools to assess our life when thrown into a hard situation. No longer do we have to believe the lies that our heroic God is far away or doesn't care or is actually the villain in the story. NO! We now see the truth, we see the father as the loving hero who rescues us and has huge plans for our lives!

Keep the right perspective on who God is, and you can rest in the boat when it's tossed by life's storms.

20 But as for you, ye thought evil against me; but God meant it unto good, to bring to pass, as it is this day, to save much people alive.

Genesis 50:20

The Scarlet Cord

Rahab was a prostitute.

She was also the great, great grandmother of King David.

An unlikely combination. To summarize her story, she is known for hiding two Jewish spies that were scouting out her land to take it as their own. These spies would eventually destroy Jericho which was her home.

Rahab and the Spies

2 And Joshua the son of Nun sent out of Shittim two men to spy secretly, saying, Go view the land, even Jericho. And they went, and came into a harlot's house, named Rahab, and lodged there.

Joshua 2:1

⁴ And the woman took the two men, and hid them, and said thus, There came men unto me, but I wist not whence they were:

⁵ And it came to pass about the time of shutting of the gate, when it was dark, that the men went out: whither the men went I wot not: pursue after them quickly; for ye shall overtake them.

⁶ But she had brought them up to the roof of the house and hid them with the stalks of flax, which she had laid in order upon the roof.

Joshua 2:4-6

²⁰ So the people shouted when the priests blew with the trumpets: and it came to pass, when the people heard the sound of the trumpet,

and the people shouted with a great shout, that the wall fell down flat, so that the people went up into the city, every man straight before him, and they took the city.

²¹ And they utterly destroyed all that was in the city, both man and woman, young and old, and ox, and sheep, and ass, with the edge of the sword.

²² But Joshua had said unto the two men that had spied out the country, Go into the harlot's house, and bring out thence the woman, and all that she hath, as ye sware unto her.

²³ And the young men that were spies went in and brought out Rahab, and her father, and her mother, and her brethren, and all that she had; and they brought out all her kindred, and left them without the camp of Israel.

Joshua 6:20-23

Rahab and her family were saved from destruction because of her decision to trust the messengers from God's chosen people.

Just as Noah and his family were saved for faithfully building the ark when there was no sign of rain.

Just as Lot and his family were saved as they ran from Sodom and Gomorrah.

Just as Joseph was saved from a pit and prison and slavery and eventually seated in power as second in command to Pharaoh of Egypt.

All these stories show us that God saves those who call on Him!

Rahab could have chosen to side with her own people instead of the spies. But Rahab knew that these two men were going to be victorious as their reputation proceeded them. Instead of relying on her tradition or culture or manmade gods, Rahab chose to believe in the God of the spies! See here how she demonstrates her faith.

⁸ And before they were laid down, she came up unto them upon the roof;

⁹ And she said unto the men, I know that the LORD hath given you the land, and that your terror is fallen upon us, and that all the inhabitants of the land faint because of you.

¹⁰ For we have heard how the LORD dried up the water of the Red sea for you, when ye came out of Egypt; and what ye did unto the two kings of the Amorites, that were on the other side Jordan, Sihon and Og, whom ye utterly destroyed.

¹¹ And as soon as we had heard these things, our hearts did melt, neither did there remain any more courage in any man, because of you: for the LORD your God, he is God in heaven above, and in earth beneath.

Joshua 2:8–11

Rahab and her family not only were saved from death but she was even added to the lineage of King David and then eventually the earthly line of Jesus. Amazing!

Another significant point to note is that Rahab had a very sordid past and yet one decision of faith changed it all. God did not look at her profession and say, "No matter how much faith you have it does not erase your past." No, not only did her decision to follow the one true God immediately nullify her sinful past but it also placed her into a line of royalty. So, this really amplifies the point that it is not our good works that bring the Father near when we are in trouble and cry out to Him. It's the mere fact that we are calling Him that He comes running.

If your child were in danger and cried out to you for help, you would not first analyze their past accomplishments or wrong choices and then decide based on that whether to come to their aid. You would come no matter what.

Rahab is just one more example of the Fathers love, and forgiveness. Also, it demonstrates his desire to rescue and redeem.

When you are staring impending doom coming your way, who will you side with? Your traditions or culture or family and friends that you are familiar with? Or the God whose reputation goes before Him? Choose wisely, it may save your life.

God's Selfie

When you snap a picture of yourself and post it on social media or send it to a friend, the idea is that you are trying to convey an image of who you are inside.

The picture could be an action shot or an up-close facial pose, depicting an emotion. When sharing the picture with others, the hope is that we are giving a message to the recipient portraying our beliefs or feelings or personality.

Jesus is, in a way, God's selfie.

What do I mean by this?

Well, Jesus was a physical manifestation of a spiritual God. Our limited vision on the earth needed some help seeing the Father.

Let's quickly examine some traits of Jesus to better picture God.

1. Jesus is compassionate

³⁵ And Jesus went about all the cities and villages, teaching in their synagogues, and preaching the gospel of the kingdom, and healing every sickness and every disease among the people.

³⁶ But when he saw the multitudes, he was moved with compassion on them, because they fainted, and were scattered abroad, as sheep having no shepherd.

Matthew 9:35-36

2. Jesus is gentle

¹³ Then were there brought unto him little children, that he should put his hands on them, and pray: and the disciples rebuked them.

¹⁴ But Jesus said, Suffer little children, and forbid them not, to come unto me: for of such is the kingdom of heaven.

¹⁵ And he laid his hands on them and departed thence.

Matthew 19:13-15

3. **Jesus is righteous**

In those days, and at that time, will I cause the Branch of righteousness to grow up unto David; and he shall execute judgment and righteousness in the land.

Jeremiah 33:15

4. Jesus has emotions

³⁹ And he came out, and went, as he was went to the mount of Olives; and his disciples also followed him. ⁴⁰ And when he was at the place, he said unto them, Pray that ye enter not into temptation. ⁴¹ And he was withdrawn from them about a stone's cast, and kneeled down, and prayed, ⁴² Saying, Father, if thou be willing, remove this cup from me: nevertheless not my will, but thine, be done. ⁴³ And there appeared an angel unto him from heaven, strengthening him. ⁴⁴ And being in agony he prayed more earnestly: and his sweat was as it were great drops of blood falling down to the ground.

Luke 22:39-44

5. Jesus keeps the law

¹⁷ "Do not think that I have come to abolish the Law or the Prophets; I have not come to abolish them but to fulfill them. ¹⁸ For truly, I say to you, until heaven and earth pass away, not an iota, not a dot, will pass from the Law until all is accomplished. ¹⁹ Therefore whoever relaxes one of the least of these commandments and teaches others to do the same will be called least in the kingdom of heaven, but whoever does them and teaches them will be called great in the kingdom of heaven.

²⁰ For I tell you unless your righteousness exceeds that of the scribes and Pharisees, you will never enter the kingdom of heaven.

Matthew 5:17-20

6. Jesus is truth

³³ Pilate then went back inside the palace, summoned Jesus and asked him, "Are you the king of the Jews?"

³⁴ "Is that your own idea," Jesus asked, "or did others talk to you about me?"

³⁵ "Am I a Jew?" Pilate replied. "Your own people and chief priests handed you over to me. What is it you have done?"

³⁶ Jesus said, "My kingdom is not of this world. If it were, my servants would fight to prevent my arrest by the Jewish leaders. But now my kingdom is from another place."

³⁷ "You are a king, then!" said Pilate.

Jesus answered, "You say that I am a king. In fact, the reason I was born and came into the world is to testify to the truth. Everyone on the side of truth listens to me."

³⁸ "What is truth?" retorted Pilate. With this, he went out again to the Jews gathered there and said, "I find no basis for a charge against him.

John 18:33-38

7. Jesus is God

¹³ When Jesus came into the coasts of Caesarea Philippi, he asked his disciples, saying, Whom do men say that I the Son of man am?

¹⁴ And they said, Some say that thou art John the Baptist: some, Elias; and others, Jeremias, or one of the prophets.

¹⁵ He saith unto them, But whom say ye that I am?

¹⁶ And Simon Peter answered and said, Thou art the Christ, the Son of the living God.

¹⁷ And Jesus answered and said unto him, Blessed art thou, Simon Barjona: for flesh and blood hath not revealed it unto thee, but my Father which is in heaven.

¹⁸ And I say also unto thee, That thou art Peter, and upon this rock, I will build my church; and the gates of hell shall not prevail against it.

¹⁹ And I will give unto thee the keys of the kingdom of heaven: and whatsoever thou shalt bind on earth shall be bound in heaven: and whatsoever thou shalt loose on earth shall be loosed in heaven.

²⁰ Then charged he his disciples that they should tell no man that he was Jesus the Christ.

Matthew 16:13-20

³⁰ I and my Father are one.

John 10:30

⁵⁸ Jesus said unto them, Verily, verily, I say unto you, Before Abraham was, I am.

John 8:58

So just by briefly examining a few verses, we can see a really great picture of what God looks like.

John 1:1 says…

8. The Word Became Flesh

In the beginning was the Word,
and the Word was with   God,   and the
Word was God.

John 1:1

Here we see the Word (another name for Jesus) was with God from the beginning and then became flesh. By becoming flesh many things were accomplished. For one, He was able to become an eternal sacrifice for all our sins so that we may one day live forever with God. This was the initial plan when Adam and Eve were created. Also, we are now able to better comprehend the love, compassion and character of the Father in heaven.

We should have known that our God is love and that he is a Hero. We see this through the stories of His people, the Jewish nation, yet we still did not seem to grasp who He is. For generation, after generation, God clearly poured blessings and favour on those who sought to know Him. Yet still, that did not fully convey Gods true nature to mankind.

Now that we see Jesus, we see the Father!

Jesus never harmed anyone.
Jesus never once turned away a single person who came to Him for healing.
Jesus wept over those he loved.
Jesus brought truth and light to a dark world.
Jesus was gentle and kind.
Jesus willingly went to His death for us.
Jesus did not force anyone to love Him. It is our free will.

So, we now have no reason to wonder about who our God is or what He is like.

Jesus shows us God!

Jesus saith unto him, Have I been so long time with you, and yet hast thou not known me, Philip? He that hath seen me hath seen the Father; and how sayest thou *then*, Shew us the Father?

John 14:9

Sleeping in the Boat

If life is crashing all around you what is your response?

Panic?

Worry?

Anger?

Or do you lay back and ride it out peacefully?

My first reactions personally, were fear, mixed with panic and worry and anger at God. This is before I learned some valuable lessons on how to respond to trouble in my life.

Why anger at God? Well, I thought even if God didn't cause the storm in my life, why allow it?

As I realized this was my reaction to life's rocky times, I began to question why this is how I felt. I came to understand that it once again went back to whether or not I believed God was good. If I could get this one issue resolved in my brain then I could rest during the trial.

So, I knew my job was to unravel the question, "Is God good?" yet again. Once I believed He was good then all I needed to do was wrestle my fleshly desire to fear, panic and worry when trouble came my way. I would need to rest in Him and resist evil.

Jesus gives us an example of how to handle a hard situation that suddenly comes upon us in the story of when he calmed a storm at sea.

23 And when he was entered into a ship, his disciples followed him.

24 And, behold, there arose a great tempest in the sea, insomuch that the ship was covered with the waves: but he was asleep.

25 And his disciples came to him, and awoke him, saying, Lord, save us: we perish.

26 And he saith unto them, Why are ye fearful, O ye of little faith? Then he arose, and rebuked the winds and the sea and there was a great calm.

27 But the men marvelled, saying, What manner of man is this, that even the winds and the sea obey him!

Matthew 8:23-27

Just picture it; you are far out in a boat, and a ferocious storm comes out of nowhere. The waves are crashing so high that they are actually sweeping over the top of your boat. This storm must have been very fierce because some of the disciples were fishermen, and even they were terrified.

How could someone sleep through this? Grown men feared their impending death at sea, and Jesus was peacefully fast asleep.

This exaggerates even more, the point that if you are in a situation where your very life is in the balance you can still be calm and at peace. Why would you be calm when things are crashing down around you? You can simply go back to the fact we discussed in the previous chapter that GOD IS GOOD! If you choose Him, He will ride out that storm right beside you. He will grant you favour, and He will deliver you from evil!

The LORD is my shepherd; I shall not want.

2 He maketh me to lie down in green pastures: he leadeth me beside the still waters.

3 He restoreth my soul: he leadeth me in the paths of righteousness for his name's sake.

⁴ Yea, though I walk through the valley of the shadow of death, I will fear no evil: for thou art with me; thy rod and thy staff they comfort me.

⁵ Thou preparest a table before me in the presence of mine enemies: thou anointest my head with oil; my cup runneth over.

⁶ Surely goodness and mercy shall follow me all the days of my life: and I will dwell in the house of the LORD for ever.

Psalm 23:1-6

When you walk through the valley of the shadow of death you need not fear evil! He is with you! He will comfort you! If you believe in the one true God and His son Jesus who He sent to save you, then you can have peace in the storm. You are not floating around, stumbling through life, one coincidence at a time. Your steps are ordered!

²³ The steps of a good man are ordered by the LORD: and he delighteth in his way.

²⁴ Though he fall, he shall not be utterly cast down: for the LORD upholdeth him with his hand.

²⁵ I have been young, and now am old; yet have I not seen the righteous forsaken, nor his seed begging bread.

Psalm 37:23-25

This verse does not say all man's steps are ordered by the Lord, it says the steps of a good man are ordered. It says the one who the Lord delights in is directed. The Lord directs the one who is righteous. We are made righteous by the blood of Jesus when we believe He was sent by the Father to rescue us from our sin. So, we have to ask ourselves, are we someone who the Lord would delight in because we obey Him? Are we righteous because we have believed in the saviour of the world, Jesus Christ? If the answers are yes, then our steps are ordered. The storm you are in is not a fluke, not a coincidence and the creator of the world is with you in it.

Psalm 23 states that God makes you lie down and rest, just as Jesus did in the boat. It says He will refresh your soul, allowing you to make it all the way through to the end. He guides you along the path for His namesake. If His name is at stake, he will surely keep your foot steady on the path that He has set out for you. He will comfort you and give you peace and rest.

So even though the outcome looks bleak. The waves are crashing down. Fear is knocking at the door. Remember....

God is not the cause, He is the answer!

Lean on him in the boat.

Rest.

Trust His goodness and know He has a good plan for your life.

Only when we know God's character, then we can truly rest in Him. When you trust someone, and you know that person is for you and has no secret motives against you, then you can completely count on them. God is more trustworthy than any human being. He adores His children and is always on their side fighting for them.

Be still and know that He makes all who love Him victorious over the storm.

¹ God is our refuge and strength, a very present help in trouble.

² Therefore will not we fear, though the earth be removed, and though the mountains be carried into the midst of the sea;

³ Though the waters thereof roar and be troubled, though the mountains shake with the swelling thereof. Selah.

⁴ There is a river, the streams whereof shall make glad the city of God, the holy place of the tabernacles of the most High.

⁵ God is in the midst of her; she shall not be moved: God shall help her, and that right early.

⁶ The heathen raged, the kingdoms were moved: he uttered his voice, the earth melted.

⁷ The LORD of hosts is with us; the God of Jacob is our refuge. Selah.

8 Come, behold the works of the LORD, what desolations he hath made in the earth.

9 He maketh wars to cease unto the end of the earth; he breaketh the bow, and cutteth the spear in sunder; he burneth the chariot in the fire.

10 Be still, and know that I am God: I will be exalted among the heathen, I will be exalted in the earth.

11 The LORD of hosts is with us; the God of Jacob is our refuge. Selah.

Psalm 46

Remember

I remember the days of old; I meditate on all thy works; I muse on the work of thy hands.

Psalm 143:5

One good way to remember something is to write it down. It's said that writing something down with a pen and paper is more helpful then typing it out.

Another good way to help your memory is to reflect on what you have just heard or read that you wish to remember.

A professor of psychology was quoted as saying that replaying memories during rest makes those earlier memories stronger. In doing so, you embed the new information into your existing knowledge.

Jewish men often wear a garment called a Tallit which is a prayer shawl. On this shawl are fringes affixed to the corners so that they would constantly remember God and His commandments. By doing this, they are able to continually jog their memory throughout the day to keep God and His laws on their mind.

What good is it to learn how much God loves us if we forget the next moment?

Many people have been greatly moved by personal encounters with the Living God and have sworn to change their lives and serve Him. Only to have that passion slowly fade as the days pass. They just forget.

Jesus gives an example of people like this in the Parable of the Sower.

³ And he spake many things unto them in parables, saying, Behold, a sower went forth to sow;

⁴ And when he sowed, some seeds fell by the wayside, and the fowls came and devoured them up:

⁵ Some fell upon stony places, where they had not much earth: and forthwith they sprung up, because they had no deepness of earth:

⁶ And when the sun was up, they were scorched; and because they had no root, they withered away.

⁷ And some fell among thorns and the thorns sprung up, and choked them:

⁸ But other fell into good ground and brought forth fruit, some a hundredfold, some sixtyfold, some thirtyfold.

⁹ Who hath ears to hear, let him hear.

Matthew 13:3-9

The seed falling on rocky ground refers to someone who hears the word and at once receives it with joy. But since they have no root, they last only a short time. When trouble or persecution comes because of the word, they quickly fall away.

So, this seems like someone who could have used a prayer shawl with memory fringes. There is a practical use in the things God commands us to do.

We can't deny we live in a distracting world. Sometimes life is too enjoyable to remember the important things of God and sometimes life seems too hard, so we get consumed by stress. Either way, this present life is just vapour that appears for a little while and then vanishes. Eternity is ETERNAL!

So how do we focus? Attention deficit issues rise as technology zooms around us. Genetically modified foods and never-ending sugar steals our ability to focus as well.

Still, God expects us to remember:

- "Remember also your Creator in the days of your youth."
- "This is my body which is for you. Do this in remembrance of me."
- "Now I commend you because you remember me in everything and maintain the traditions even as I delivered them to you."
- "Then take care lest you forget the LORD, who brought you out of the land of Egypt, out of the house of slavery."
- "This cup is the new covenant in my blood. Do this, as often as you drink it, in remembrance of me."
- "Remember the Sabbath day, to keep it holy."

The Lord knows we can forget all the wonderful things He does for us. Since we know that there are practical ways to increase the chance of us keeping the essential things fresh in our minds than why not implement them.

For instance, you can write down a sentence and keep it in a special place that describes a time or times, when God has rescued you. This sentence can be your fringe and can quickly bring to mind who God is. When lies bombard us and tell us that our Father is something other than good, we can say, "No, not true. I remember!"

One idea is to DIY a bookmark with the reminder sentence on it and keep it handy in your bible. Adding thread at the top can be another reminder of the prayer shawl and fringes.

As I mentioned previously, reflecting on the thing we wish to remember strengthens this memory in our brain. So, don't just read the sentence you write on the bookmark, reflect on it for a moment. Society is big on meditation, and God was the one who thought that up first. The bible says blessed is the one who meditates on God's word day and night. As you remember the moment from your bookmark, pause and visualize the scene. Let it sink deep into your mind to strengthen the memory of how God rescued you.

God also commanded the Israelites to build memorials. This word memorial means "to remember".

A few examples of Memorials God commanded are:

- The Lord's super to remember Christ's sacrifice.
- Passover Feast to remember the Lord sparing Israel from the hand of death.
- The rainbow after the flood.
- The Sabbath day to remind of the deliverance from slavery in Egypt and to remember that God also rested on the last day of creation.

There are many good things to remember from the Bible. First, I suggest trying the bookmark trick. This small memorial provides a basis to remember that GOD IS GOOD! Once that fact is firmly established in your brain then you can view everything else through the correct lens.

Keep in mind that God never forgets you as His child. He declares that He will remember your sins no more when you put them all on Jesus but you, He never forgets!

Behold, I have graven thee upon the palms of my hands; thy walls are continually before me.

Isaiah 49:16

Promise Keeper

Kids love when their parents keep their word. If a parent promises a trip out after dinner to get ice cream, you can bet they will hold you to it. When a parent breaks their promises, the child learns that the father or mother is not fully trustworthy. Slowly that lack of trust turns into disrespect. Then eventually the child stops asking for things knowing there is no reason to get their hopes up only to be disappointed in the end.

Is that what God is like? The God of Abraham Isaac and Jacob? A promise breaker? Untrustworthy?

Were any promises made to these three men, and were they kept?

Let's first look at Abraham…

2 And I will make of thee a great nation, and I will bless thee, and make thy name great, and thou shalt be a blessing:

³ And I will bless them that bless thee, and curse him that curseth thee: and in thee shall all families of the earth be blessed.

genesis 12:2-3

And...

In the same day, the LORD made a covenant with Abram, saying, Unto thy seed have I given this land, from the river of Egypt unto the great river, the river Euphrates.

Genesis 15:18

At the time not only did Abraham not possess these lands but he also had no children and was a very old man! So, keeping this promise seemed unlikely, to say the least.

Eventually, Abraham did have two sons. Isaac, Abraham's youngest continued in the promise given to his father. This is what God promised Isaac…

3 Sojourn in this land and I will be with thee, and will bless thee; for unto thee, and unto thy seed, I will give all these countries, and I will perform the oath which I sware unto Abraham thy father;

4 And I will make thy seed to multiply as the stars of heaven, and will give unto thy seed all these countries; and in thy seed shall all the nations of the earth be blessed;

5 Because that Abraham obeyed my voice, and kept my charge, my commandments, my statutes, and my laws.

Genesis 26:3-5

The complete promise had not yet come to pass in the natural, but it was in the works. Abraham did have a seed, and that seed was blessed and multiplied. God did not say to Abraham that he will see the Promised Land, but he said that Abraham's decedents would be given the land.

Isaac's son Jacob had his grandfather's promise from God confirmed as well.

13 And, behold, the LORD stood above it, and said, I am the LORD God of Abraham thy father, and the God of Isaac: the land whereon thou liest, to thee will I give it, and to thy seed;

14 And thy seed shall be as the dust of the earth, and thou shalt spread abroad to the west, and to the east, and to the north, and to the south: and in thee and in thy seed shall all the families of the earth be blessed.

¹⁵ And, behold, I am with thee, and will keep thee in all places whither thou goest, and will bring thee again into this land; for I will not leave thee, until I have done that which I have spoken to thee of.

Genesis 28:13-15

This was a tremendous promise which took generations to accomplish. Eventually, the land described was indeed given to Abrahams decedents.

This brings us to the conclusion that God is not the kind of Father that goes back on His word. He can be trusted!

The way we can apply this in our everyday life is by trusting God's word. We can look at numerous verses that promise wonderful things to those who choose Him. Just a few promises are…

- Nothing can separate us from Gods love. Romans 8:38-39

- If you believe in Jesus as God's son, you will live forever in heaven John 3:16

- God wants to prosper you and not harm you. Jeremiah 29:11

If we know that God is faithful to keep His promises then we can rest in that. If we are afraid or sad or hurting, then we can follow these steps to reassure our hearts and minds that it's going to be ok.

1. Remember God did not bring evil upon you. He is not the cause.

2. Jesus is showing you the Father's character which is good.

3. Remember the times that God rescued His children in the past.

4. Read promises in the bible and know that He is faithful.

5. Encourage yourself that Jesus went to prepare an eternal home for us. We will be given new imperishable bodies and a new home.

Try going through this short list the next time trouble hits. Nip the lies in the bud. God has beautiful promises for you, and He always keeps them!

So shall my word be that goeth forth out of my mouth: it shall not return unto me void, but it shall accomplish that which I please, and it shall prosper in the thing whereto I sent it.

Isaiah 55:11

The Great Escape

The whole reason I wrote this book is to try to show others that God is good. That may seem like a silly statement, but it was something I struggled with greatly. When trials came my way, I noticed that I was angry with God. I had never firmly established deep down that God is the hero, not the villain.

Hopefully, by this point you are feeling much more confident in the goodness of God. Some may argue that if He were so good there would be no trouble or pain and God would intervene more often. Trouble and pain weren't the initial plan for mankind. We know that in the beginning God created man and woman and placed them in a beautiful garden full of every good plant to eat. They had no knowledge of evil. They were given a choice, and that's where things went downhill. They chose to know evil.

Some may say that it would have been better to limit that choice and keep the pair as obedient children with no options. One issue with this is that God by nature is relational. We are told He is three in One. Father, Son and Holy Spirit. This trinity interacts within itself. I don't claim to understand it all, but it is clear that God is relational. The bible says that God walked with man in the cool of the day in the garden. This again illustrates the desire for a relationship with man. Not a robotic being without choice.

All throughout scripture we see that those who walked and talked with God were the ones He called His own. These people understood that God wanted us to be in a loving relationship with him from day one. He wanted to provide for all our needs. We were to worship, love an obey Him, and He would eternally love us back. Since the choice to know evil was made by man, the intimate bond was fractured.

But God was not done with the plan! He knew that throughout history there would be people who would love Him. He would call people out of idol worship and reveal His truth to them, and some would reject the truth, but some would accept it and believe! These believers throughout history would create the family that God desired from day one. God did not need this companionship, but it was another way to bring Him glory. So, the big plan continued.

After Adam and Eve left the close connection with God in the Garden of Eden a distance between man and God grew over the generations. Life was hard, and the memory of God began to fade. Eventually, Abraham was called out of paganism and shown who the true creator of the world really was. Not the gold and wooden statues that he had been taught had created the earth. Instead of a dead, unfeeling, manmade statue, he found a God who talked with him, blessed him, and showed him the truth.

Through Abraham's line, the Jewish nation, the world would see the real Creator. The God of Israel would conquer and prosper against all odds. They would be a peculiar people, called out from the nations. They would not worship false gods as the other nations did. They declared that their God was the one true creator of heaven and earth and that all the other stone, metal and wood gods were false.

So, the plan to redeem mankind proceeded along. When Jesus was born this changed everything. Previously the Jewish nation was told to live by many laws. They sacrificed animals to symbolically pay for their sins. This law and sacrifice illuminated the fact that man could do nothing without God and that there was no way to earn His love and provision. This was a symbolic act of repentance.

Jesus would then be the final sacrifice for all sin. Those who believed that He was the picture of God on earth would be grafted back into the family of God. The redemption plan was complete.

A verse that helps bring this point home is found in a conversation between Jesus and a Samaritan woman. Samaritans were actually off-limits to a Jewish person especially a Samaritan woman! The Jews did not associate with them. Jesus upheld Gods law, but man's law was a different story. God's law was put in place to magnify sin. Jesus did not break God's law by talking with this woman He only amplified God's love for the world. Jesus reveals to the woman that the family whom God desires is on its way.

22 Ye worship ye know not what: we know what we worship: for salvation is of the Jews.

23 But the hour cometh, and now is, when the true worshippers shall worship the Father in spirit and in truth: for the Father seeketh such to worship him.

John 4:22-23

Jesus says salvation came from the Jews, but the true worshipers will come from all over now. The Jews were examples, but now Jesus is the final example. This verse also says these true worshipers are the ones the Father wants to worship Him. Not mindless followers but children of the light! This is the family He desires!

Where does that leave us now?

The main point of this book is to focus on bringing to light the true Heroic nature of God. God was not done with His rescue mission. He rescues until this earth passes away.

Jesus told His disciples that He was going to prepare a place for them just before He ascended up to heaven. His disciples had always been curious about the end of the world and the afterlife. They wanted to know where Jesus was going, where they would end up and how it would all go down. These are valid questions in my opinion. Let's read more about this end time.

The Signs of the Times and the End of the Age

³ Now as He sat on the Mount of Olives, the disciples came to Him privately, saying, "Tell us, when will these things be? And what *will be* the sign of Your coming, and of the end of the age?"

⁴ And Jesus answered and said to them: "Take heed that no one deceives you. ⁵ For many will come in My name, saying, 'I am the Christ,' and will deceive many. ⁶ And you will hear of wars and rumors of wars. See that you are not troubled; for all *these things* must come to pass, but the end is not yet. ⁷ For nation will rise against nation, and kingdom against kingdom. And there will be famines, pestilences, and earthquakes in various places. ⁸ All these *are* the beginning of sorrows.

⁹ "Then they will deliver you up to tribulation and kill you, and you will be hated by all nations for My name's sake. ¹⁰ And then many will be offended, will betray one another, and will hate one another. ¹¹ Then many false prophets will rise up and deceive many. ¹² And because lawlessness will abound, the love of many will grow cold. ¹³ But he who endures to the end shall be saved. ¹⁴ And this gospel of the kingdom will be preached in all the world as a witness to all the nations, and then the end will come.

The Great Tribulation

15 "Therefore when you see the 'abomination of desolation,' spoken of by Daniel the prophet, standing in the holy place" (whoever reads, let him understand), 16 "then let those who are in Judea flee to the mountains. 17 Let him who is on the housetop not go down to take anything out of his house. 18 And let him who is in the field not go back to get his clothes. 19 But woe to those who are pregnant and to those who are nursing babies in those days! 20 And pray that your flight may not be in winter or on the Sabbath. 21 For then there will be great tribulation, such as has not been since the beginning of the world until this time, no, nor ever shall be. 22 And unless those days were shortened, no flesh would be saved; but for the elect's sake those days will be shortened.

²³ "Then if anyone says to you, 'Look, here *is* the Christ!' or 'There!' do not believe *it*. ²⁴ For false christs and false prophets will rise and show great signs and wonders to deceive, if possible, even the elect. ²⁵ See, I have told you beforehand.

²⁶ "Therefore if they say to you, 'Look, He is in the desert!' do not go out; *or* 'Look, *He is* in the inner rooms!' do not believe *it*. ²⁷ For as the lightning comes from the east and flashes to the west, so also will the coming of the Son of Man be. ²⁸ For wherever the carcass is, there the eagles will be gathered together.

The Coming of the Son of Man

29 "Immediately after the tribulation of those days the sun will be darkened, and the moon will not give its light; the stars will fall from heaven, and the powers of the heavens will be shaken. 30 Then the sign of the Son of Man will appear in heaven, and then all the tribes of the earth will mourn, and they will see the Son of Man coming on the clouds of heaven with power and great glory. 31 And He will send His angels with a great sound of a trumpet, and they will gather together His elect from the four winds, from one end of heaven to the other.

Matthew 24:3-31

These verses describe the end of the world. The events, in a nutshell, are that there will be many signs as described above that will be the early "birth pains" followed by more intense signs, just as the labour of a baby intensifies in the end. There will be devastation all over the earth. The earth itself will be in labour with intense natural disasters. Evil beings will be on earth. There will be tribulation as never before. After the appointed time of wrath is over, then Jesus will return to the earth not as a baby like in Bethlehem but as a conquering king!

How is this heroic you may ask? This seems quite the opposite. It seems horrible. There is a part of the story that is found sprinkled throughout scripture. This is known as the catching away of the church. Not a church building but church meaning the followers of Jesus. The family of God, the true worshipers God desired. Here are some verses describing this event called the catching away. Another word Christians use is 'the rapture'. This word is not found in the bible, but it is a descriptive word for the event that rescues the church from the end time wrath of God.

Watch ye therefore, and pray always, that ye may be accounted worthy to escape all these things that shall come to pass, and to stand before the Son of man

Luke 21:36

⁵¹ Behold, I shew you a mystery; We shall not all sleep, but we shall all be changed,

⁵² In a moment, in the twinkling of an eye, at the last trump: for the trumpet shall sound, and the dead shall be raised incorruptible, and we shall be changed.

⁵³ For this corruptible must put on incorruption, and this mortal must put on immortality.

1 Corinthians 15:51-53

¹⁶ For the Lord himself shall descend from heaven with a shout, with the voice of the archangel, and with the trump of God: and the dead in Christ shall rise first:

¹⁷ Then we which are alive and remain shall be caught up together with them in the clouds, to meet the Lord in the air: and so shall we ever be with the Lord.

¹⁸ Wherefore comfort one another with these words.

1 Thessalonians 4:16–18

³⁴ I tell you, in that night there shall be two men in one bed; the one shall be taken, and the other shall be left.

³⁵ Two women shall be grinding together; the one shall be taken, and the other left.

³⁶ Two men shall be in the field; the one shall be taken, and the other left.

Luke 17:34–36

³⁷ But as the days of Noah were, so shall also the coming of the Son of man be.

³⁸ For as in the days that were before the flood they were eating and drinking, marrying and giving in marriage, until the day that Noah entered into the ark,

³⁹ And knew not until the flood came, and took them all away so shall also the coming of the Son of man be.

Matthew 24 37:39

So, we see here that there will be a time when people are going about daily life as usual as in the days of Noah, and then the Tribulation will come upon them surprisingly. We see there will be two in the field working or two in bed sleeping, and one will be taken away and one left. We hear that the moment the person is taken they will be changed in the twinkling of an eye to a new body. Lastly, we see that God has mercifully said He will keep His church from the wrath to come upon the whole earth. He will keep the church from the hour of trial testing the world.

People have argued that because this rescue known as the rapture isn't spelled out specifically but only eluded to in verses scattered through the bible that this is an untrue event. I wrestled with that myself as I didn't want to be swayed by false teachings but only following the true words of the bible. What convinced me was that the wrath described by Jesus poured out on the earth is very obvious. At that time, it is not daily life as usual. It will be pure chaos. But we are taken when people are still getting married, and working in the field, and living life as usual. They will not be fleeing from meteors, earthquakes, hail, and persecution from the antichrist. So, this event must be prior. Also, we are told we will be kept from this time of wrath as I stated above in the book of Revelation. This is repeated here in the letter to the Thessalonians.

9 For God hath not appointed us to wrath, but to obtain salvation by our Lord Jesus Christ.

1 Thessalonians 5:9

We are also told to pray that we are kept from this time of wrath. This has sprung the debate that not all believers will be caught up before the great tribulation. That is not my main point here, but it is interesting to note that we are told to pray about this.

^{36} Watch ye therefore, and pray always, that ye may be accounted worthy to escape all these things that shall come to pass, and to stand before the Son of man.

Luke 21:36

So we see it is not God's plan to test us as the rest of the world will be tested. We have already lived in a world that didn't believe and we did not give in to that temptation. We were told to pray that we can escape the coming wrath.

God mercifully showed me that this was another big rescue act and I wanted in! Just as Noah escaped the flood, we will escape the coming tribulation.

Even if the last flight out of Dodge has taken off, hope is still not lost! The bible says that anyone who believes in Him and declares that Jesus is Lord will be saved from the second death which is hell. This person living in the tribulation must not take the mark that is mandated by the antichrist. This is the final way to show allegiance to the one true God!

⁹ And the third angel followed them, saying with a loud voice, If any man worship the beast and his image, and receive his mark in his forehead, or in his hand,

¹⁰ The same shall drink of the wine of the wrath of God, which is poured out without mixture into the cup of his indignation; and he shall be tormented with fire and brimstone in the presence of the holy angels, and in the presence of the Lamb:

¹¹ And the smoke of their torment ascendeth up for ever and ever: and they have no rest day nor night, who worship the beast and his image, and whosoever receiveth the mark of his name.

Revelation 14:9–11

⁹ The Lord is not slack concerning his promise, as some men count slackness; but is longsuffering to us-ward, not willing that any should perish, but that all should come to repentance.

2 Peter 3:9

In Conclusion, our God saves!

He rescues!

He prepared a place for His family to live with Him forever.

Jesus shows us the Father.

He is Good!

We are loved, protected and rescued from sin and death. In our daily lives, we can talk to God because that's what he always wanted. One day the family of God will be together forever in a home that was made perfectly for us. If this world was made in seven days what must our new home be like which has been in the making for over 2000 years?

Join the family of God. Know He is on your side and that he will never leave you or forsake you. Believe that he is good and His promises are true!

Let Him be your HERO!

RESCUED

Fear thou not; for I am with thee: be not dismayed; for I am thy God: I will strengthen thee; yea, I will help thee; yea, I will uphold thee with the right hand of my righteousness.

REDEEMED

For God so loved the world, that he gave his only begotten Son, that whosoever believeth in him should not perish, but have everlasting life.

REMEMBERED

Behold, I have graven thee upon the palms of my hands; thy walls are continually before me.

Made in the USA
Middletown, DE
13 March 2019